Zoom In on Savanna Animals

Cheetahs

Leo Statts

abdopublishing.com

Published by Abdo Zoom™, PO Box 398166, Minneapolis, Minnesota 55439. Copyright © 2017 by Abdo Consulting Group, Inc. International copyrights reserved in all countries. No part of this book may be reproduced in any form without written permission from the publisher. Abdo Zoom™ is a trademark and logo of Abdo Consulting Group, Inc.

Printed in the United States of America, North Mankato, Minnesota
062016
092016

 THIS BOOK CONTAINS
RECYCLED MATERIALS

Cover Photo: JMx Images/Shutterstock Images
Interior Photos: Eric Isselée/iStockphoto, 1; Dirk Freder/iStockphoto, 4; iStockphoto, 5, 10–11, 13, 15 (top), 15 (bottom), 16, 19; Jonathan C Photography/Shutterstock Images, 6; Kally Hall/iStockphoto, 7; W. L. Davies/iStockphoto, 8; Gudkov Andrey/Shutterstock Images, 9, 17; Red Line Editorial, 11, 20 (left), 20 (right), 21 (left), 21 (right); Johan Barnard/Shutterstock Images, 12–13; Hansjoerg Richter/iStockphoto, 14; Christoffer Vorm/iStockphoto, 18

Editor: Emily Temple
Series Designer: Madeline Berger
Art Direction: Dorothy Toth

Publisher's Cataloging-in-Publication Data
Names: Statts, Leo, author.
Title: Cheetahs / by Leo Statts.
Description: Minneapolis, MN : Abdo Zoom, [2017] | Series: Savanna animals |
    Includes bibliographical references and index.
Identifiers: LCCN 2016941190 | ISBN 9781680791990 (lib. bdg.) |
    ISBN 9781680793673 (ebook) | ISBN 9781680794564 (Read-to-me ebook)
Subjects: LCSH: Cheetahs--Juvenile literature.
Classification: DDC 599.75--dc23
LC record available at http://lccn.loc.gov/2016941190

Table of Contents

Cheetahs

Cheetahs are big cats.

They are
fast runners.
Cheetahs are the
fastest animals
on land.

Cheetahs have long tails.
The tails help them steer
while running.

They have stripes on their tails.

They have light brown fur. It has black spots. They have **markings** by their eyes.

It looks like they have tears
running down their faces.

Habitat

Cheetahs live in Africa. They live in Asia. You can find them in the grassy plains. They also live in open savannas.

☐ Where cheetahs live

Food

Cheetahs are meat eaters.

They hunt in the day.
Most other big cats hunt at night.

After a cheetah catches
its prey, it waits to eat.
It needs to catch its breath.

Cheetahs eat gazelles.

They also eat antelopes.

Life Cycle

Female cheetahs have
two to five babies at a time.

The babies are called cubs.

Mothers hide their cubs. This keeps them safe from **predators**.

Cheetahs usually live
for 10 to 12 years.

Average Speed

A cheetah is as fast as a car on a highway.

70 mph   70 mph

Average Length

A cheetah is longer than an acoustic guitar.

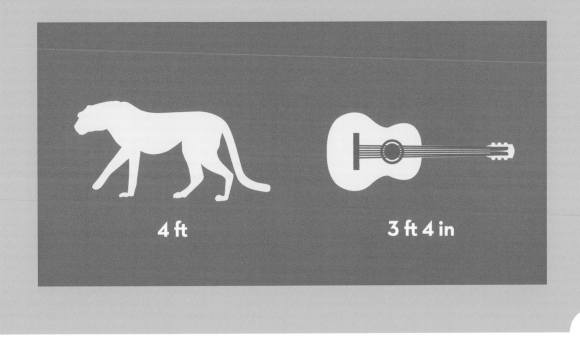

4 ft

3 ft 4 in

Glossary

cub - a young animal.

marking - a mark or pattern of marks on an animal's fur.

plain - an area of dry, grassy land.

predator - an animal that hunts others.

prey - an animal hunted or killed by a predator for food.

savanna - a grassland with few or no trees.

Booklinks

For more information
on **cheetahs**, please visit
booklinks.abdopublishing.com

Z👁m In on Animals!

Learn even more with the Abdo Zoom
Animals database. Check out
abdozoom.com for more information.

Index